GIVE YOURSELF PERMISSION TO BE HAPPY EVERYDAY

" How you feel is determined by how you think you feel. If you think you're happy, you will be; if you expect good things to happen, they will. "

When we love someone, we see
the best of who we are in them,
and we are inspired to be
even better.

" Sometimes a person doesn't have much faith in themselves, but a loved one has faith enough to fill the gaps. "

Love

without
conditions

"To love me is not to understand everything about me, but to want to."

LOVE
ALLOWS ANOTHER
TO FLY FREE

"Loving sometimes means holding on, and sometimes letting go. Trust your heart to know the time for each."

Teaching shares hearts and minds.

“ Fill young minds with knowledge;
fill young hearts with hope. ”

A New Day Is a New Opportunity . . .

"With wisdom and knowledge to guide you, let this day be a whole new start to live the life you've dreamed of."

Never underestimate the
power of a loving touch.

"Thinking of our own needs is natural. Thinking of what others need is supernatural."

Knowledge is what separates being prepared from being lucky.

" Admitting a mistake is just the first small step. Learning from it requires a great leap. "

live life in full BLOOM

" If you want to conquer the anxiety of life, live in the moment, live in the breath. "

A CALM SPIRIT
POURS WATER ON
THE HOTTEST FIRE.

" *Forgiveness is the first step on the road to a fresh start.* "

PRACTICE ALTRUISM EVERY DAY

“ Enhance your own spiritual growth by contributing to the growth of others. ”

KEEP YOUR EXPECTATIONS **HIGH** AND YOUR VOICE **LOW.**

"All it takes to triumph over adversity is the conviction that you can."

give thanks

for every moment

" Our most cherished moments are eternal. We treasure them as they occur and savor them over and over again as beloved memories. "

EMBRACE YOUR INDIVIDUALITY

" As hard as you may try to fit in,
the times when you most comfortably
'fit' are when you are yourself. "

A compassionate act
is often its own reward.

" Patience is often a simple matter of putting yourself in another's place. "

Posterity will prosper

"The greatest achievements of your life begin the moment you take the wisdom and knowledge you have gained and go out into the world to share it with others."

STEP BOLDLY INTO THE FUTURE

" Success comes to those who have proceeded to do what the rest of us have always intended to do. Without great risks there can be no great rewards. "

Trust your IMAGINATION and follow it

“ Creative people don’t have more ideas than other people. They have merely learned to recognize them. ”

Wisdom relies on common sense and uncommon thoughts.

"When you open your mind instead of your mouth, you'll see the open doors more clearly."

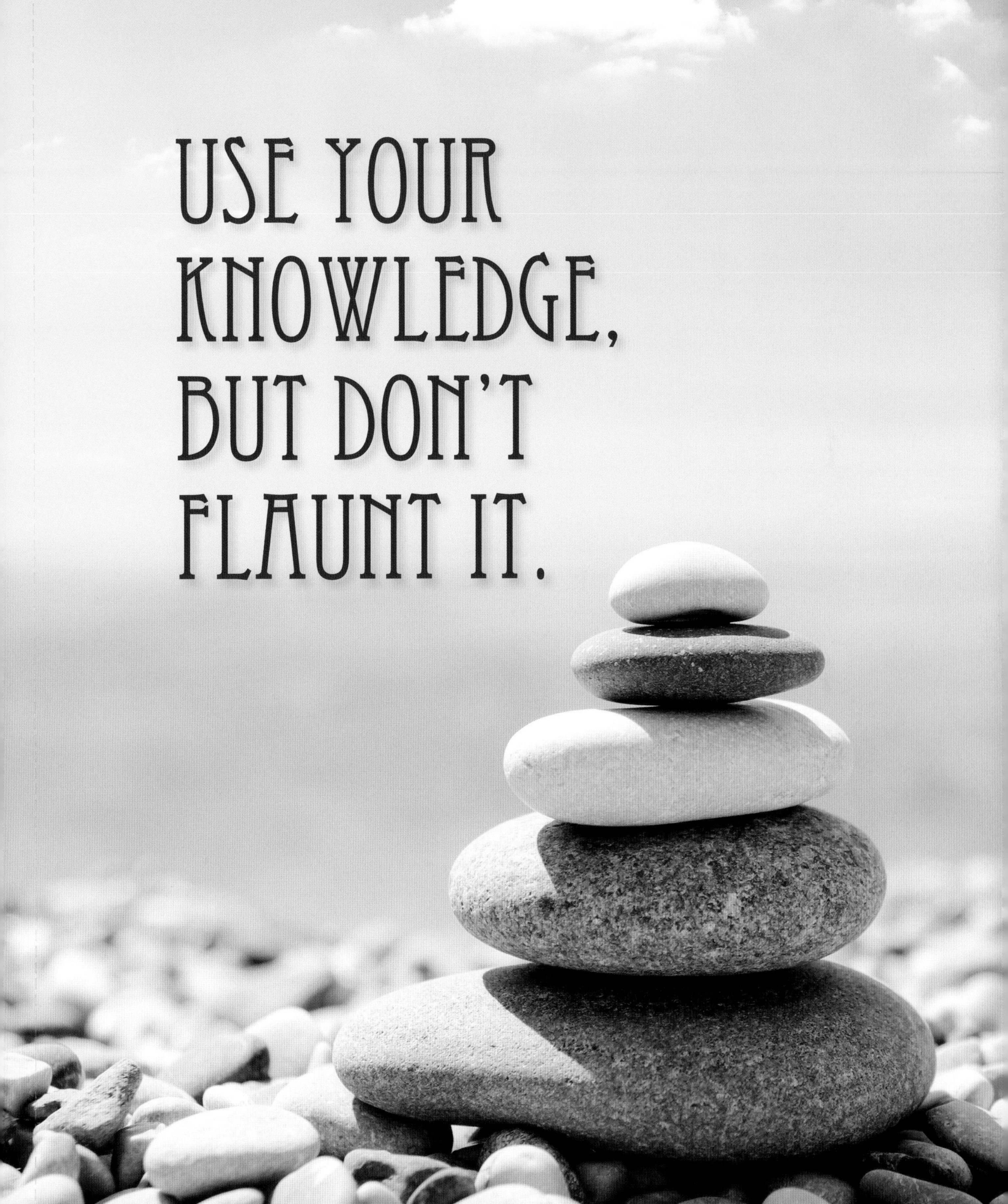
USE YOUR
KNOWLEDGE,
BUT DON'T
FLAUNT IT.

" Growing in wisdom means growing in love, tolerance, grace, and acceptance. "

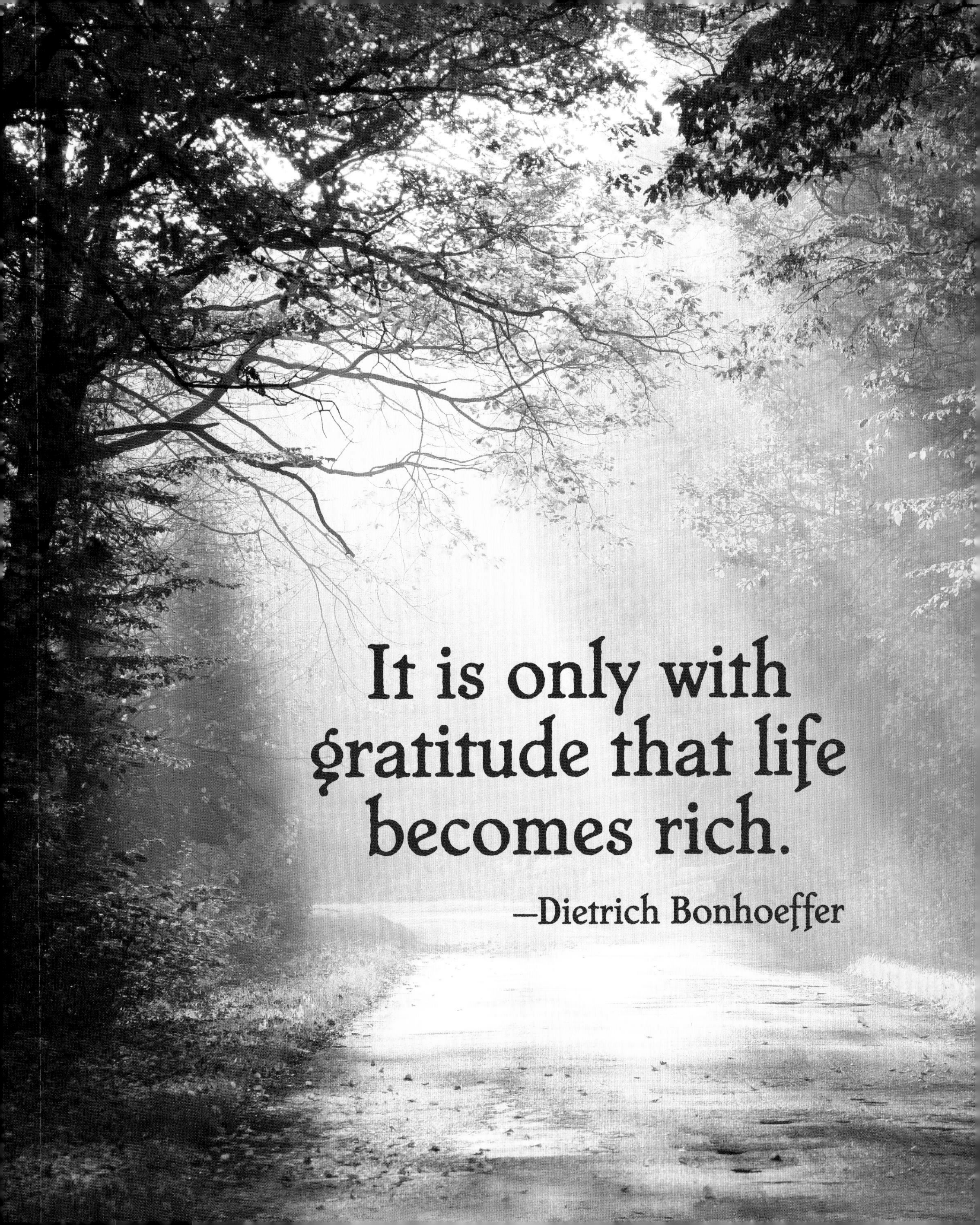
It is only with
gratitude that life
becomes rich.
—Dietrich Bonhoeffer

“ You have the power to make happiness a way of life instead of an occasional experience. ”

YOU
DO
YOU

"What does humility mean?
It doesn't mean you should look down on yourself, but that you should accept yourself for who you are, including the good and the bad."

SILENCE
SPEAKS
VOLUMES

" It is so comforting to walk into a room and have someone understand my silence. "

ALL TEACHERS WERE ONCE STUDENTS.

“The best thing about learning is that someday we may teach others what we know.”

Wherever you are in life,
a turning point is just ahead.

" Step off the obvious path once in a while; it may not be a shortcut or an easy route, but the scenery will make your journey twice as beautiful. "

BE
RESILIENT

" The resilient heart withstands the winds of change, just as the flexible branch of a tree bends but does not break. "

Love depends
on what you do,
not how you feel.

" Caring for another, by its very nature, involves risk. But what better risk to take than to love, for the returns are unequaled. "

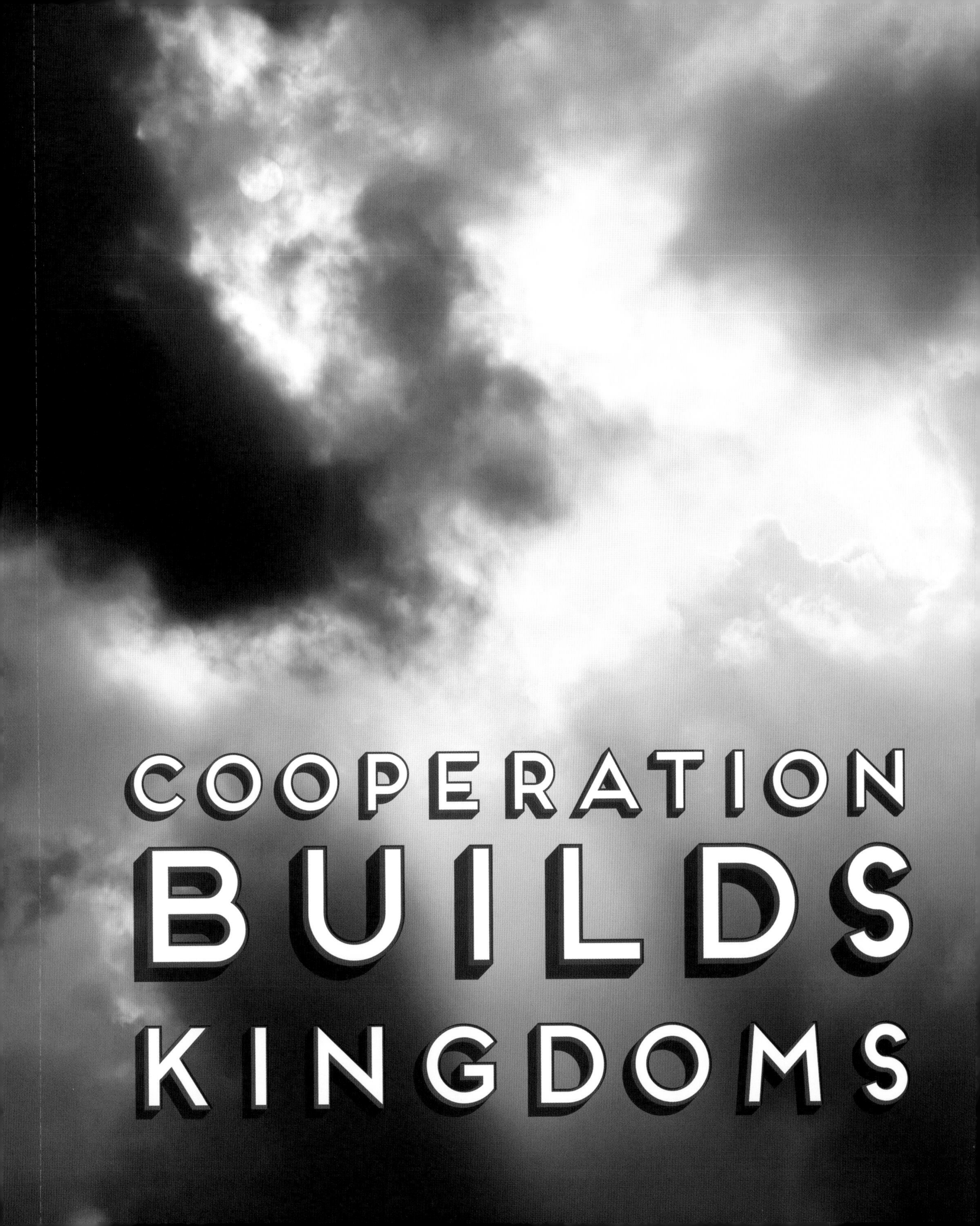

COOPERATION
BUILDS
KINGDOMS

" If we want peace with others, we need to let go of self-interest. Only then does peace become possible. "

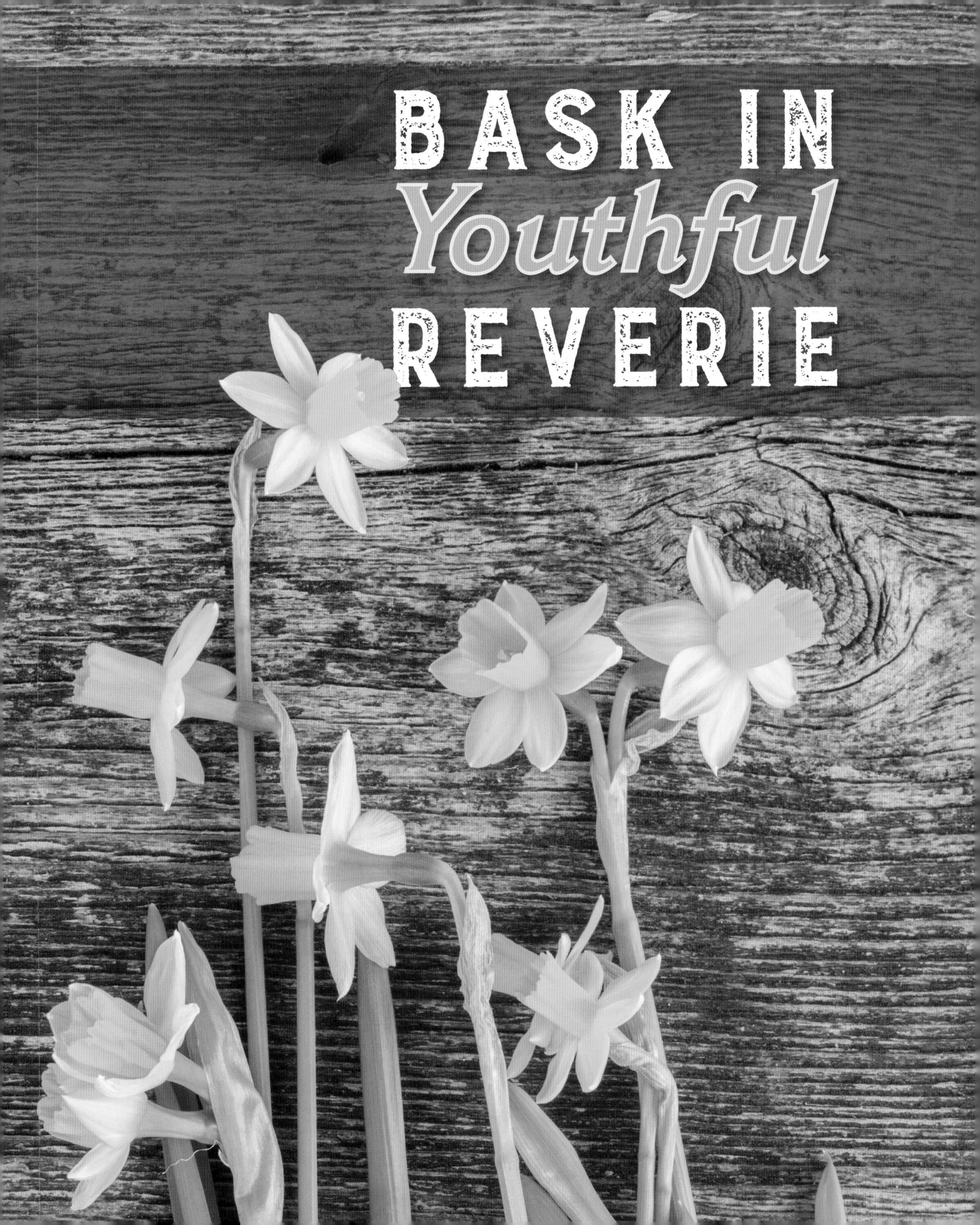
BASK IN
Youthful
REVERIE

" Many a new thought, called forth when we're grown, turns out to have sprung from a dream of our youth. "

VIRTUE
IS UBIQUITOUS

"Those who choose to see the good in people will be comforted by the goodness that abounds."

NATURE HEALS ALL

" Surround yourself with the serenity of nature, and you will feel more at peace with yourself and the world. "

LIVE
THE
DREAM
EVERY
DAY

" Hold on to your dreams; they will help guide you on your own path to happiness. "

Each moment is
an opportunity
to do good.

" It is not the challenges we face that make us stronger; it is how we handle them. "

Only you can describe how you feel.

" No one can make you feel anything—
you have to cooperate. "

LAUGH EVERY DAY

" Humor is proof of humanity's ability to overcome adversity. "

CONFIRM YOUR WORDS WITH ACTIONS.

" A person of integrity is not one who never does anything wrong, but one who is grieved each time they do and desire to make things right. "

REMAIN RECEPTIVE TO WHAT THE WORLD GIVES YOU.

"The simple words 'I do' represent enough sentences, paragraphs, and pages to fill an entire library."

Show us
what you can do.

"It is important that a wise person passes on their wisdom—not only in words, but in deeds."

CREATE

LOVE

" The beauty of creation inspires
me to live a life where I, too,
can create something beautiful. "

Tolerance
unites

" Tolerance is not about acknowledging people and accepting their beliefs; rather, it is just the opposite—accepting people and acknowledging their beliefs. "